# Cast Iron

# Omissions

Janate' "Solar" Ingram

SS Still Standing
Publishing Company

Creative Direction: Janate Ingram, Bernadine C. Taylor, Tamiko Lowry-Pugh

Edited by Bernadine C. Taylor

Published by Printed and bound in the United States of America

First edition

ISBN-13: 978-1543070217

# Dedication

In Loving Memory… Robert L. Ingram
My Little Brother…. Rob
July 31, 1988 – March 19, 2013
Though I lost you due to a house fire for which you could not
escape in time….You prepared me for what lied ahead. You told
me what I needed to get there, how, when and why….Who I
needed to take with me and who I needed to leave behind….
Still Missing You Lil' Bro!

# Acknowledgements

To God Be The Glory for the work He has wrought in my life. Without Him, none of this would be possible. God is the source of my everything. In Him, I live, move and have my being…

To my four sons, and two grandsons, at the time of this work, "My Life, My reason for living,"

Terrance, TeJohn, Khalid, Christopher, Terrance, Jr. and Tyron Without you, I would not have survived!!

5

To My Zee
Cauenusa.

Thank You
So much
for Your
Energy.

Much
Love & Dancing!

XO
The Corvettes
Daughter

# Table of Contents

**Foreword**

# FOREWORD

Cast Iron Omissions is a deep spiritual encounter between the Author and the Creator of Mankind. It bears the true essence of her innermost thoughts and aspirations to achieving spiritual success and guidance that is needed in a world that can seem to be against you at times. Through her trials and tribulations, she has expressed how important it is that your life is lined up with God's will and what you may have planned for your future, God will shake it all up so that you will acknowledge and obey Him first.

Deeply embedded in this never before told story is a remarkable transformation of a victim of not only child rape, and domestic violence (that led to promiscuity), but alcoholism, depression, failed relationships and marriages all for the purpose to derive at that one ultimate victory of "peace within."

Cast Iron Omissions also chronologically depicts the struggle of the Author's ability to withstand obstacles as her secular and spiritual worlds collide and at times appear that she would be knocked out by the blows coming from all angles; in retrospect to teach others that *it is possible to STAY STRONG in the midst of adversities*.

As you read, you will experience episodes that the Author tried numerous times to omit, thus became seared as 'Cast Iron' rooted in her soul… that subsequently produced a resilience that only she could conquer and convey.

This Memoir will make you wiser, prouder and determined not to go down certain paths in life that were not designed for you to take on. But only the paths that God created for you to travel from the beginning with the hopes of escaping pitfalls, mishaps, and agony to bring hope, joy, love and restoration to your family. As the excerpt also clearly defines the Author's true sentiments of her heart....

*"Never would have made it without you, yes you Lord!*

*I'm stronger because I stepped out on faith.*

*All of a sudden, I'm wiser because first I sought your face,*

*Oh God! I'm better because I know that the plan you have for my life is good, all good!"*

*"And He gave some, Apostles; and some, Prophets;*

*and some, Evangelists; and some Pastors and Teachers;*

*for perfecting of the Saints, for the work of the Ministry,*

*for the edifying of the Body of Christ:*

*Til we all come in the unity of the faith,*

*and the knowledge of the Son of God,*

*unto a perfect man, unto the measure*

*of the stature of the fullness of Christ."*

*Ephesians 4:11-13*

***Evangelist*** *– One who proclaims good news.*

***Evangelism*** *– Proclaiming the Gospel to those that have not heard or received it.*

# PROLOGUE

## Evangelism

**The Calling God placed on my life**... It was foretold at the time of my birth that a special child would be born. A *Prophet* informed my Parents that I would speak *truth* to many. Even more so... that my life was already spoken for and God had prepared a path for me that would be magnetic to all those whom I'd encounter. As a child, I even heard the *voice of God*, indeed, yet was unable to answer. I was about six years old. My parents were separated, and I was sent to Alabama with *unfamiliar* family members.

After a series of abusive nights and lonely days, I prayed that God would take me back to New York with my Father, at least until my Mother finished college. The answer came in the form of a telephone number... a number that I learned well before I left home... *my Grandparents*, I knew it like it was a social security number, like the back of my hand, and better than my birthday. Yes, til this day, by God's grace, I recall the number that I was able to remember; never realizing I would need to use it when in dire straits.

Yet, my spiritual *"Calling"* still had not been put to work, although there were early warning signs that taught me how to handle situations whenever I asked God to get involved. Being misguided, however, disallowed me to adhere to hardly anything. In my awkwardness, I just told my family who I was *entrusted* to whenever questioned about my behavior, that I was more comfortable being around people I knew; trying to never become bitter or negative about my mistreatment. I even told my new found family that I was *thankful* to be living with them, (out of fear of persecution) and that I really missed my Father, *in which I did.*

On the other hand, my Mother, who attended Alabama State University, began to feel betrayed for letting me stay with them. I found myself reassuring her, that she felt that way, *"because God wanted me to go back home, it was my time to leave; not hers."*

A walk in the light has never been and will never be easy, but *God knows.* Still, I knew early on that if I would endure all the hardship, abandonment, rape, wrong decisions, and other means of ungodly treatment, then something was definitely in the storehouse with my name on it.

As a teenager, I, like most youth who has been taught the difference between right and wrong, experienced the attack of the enemy and went contrary. Thoughts of suicide, a dance with alcohol, and an addiction to smoking marijuana were my safe havens. My philosophy was that if I could get drunk, I could numb the pain of feeling alone, and if I had sex, I would feel as if I was loved. Then I could block out the dreams that I was having on a regular basis. Oxymoron at its best!

Yet, contrary to popular belief, when I was under the influence of controlled substances, I produced more... I wrote more... *poetry with an edge of truth unseen.* I would study and pass my exams, and I was able to tell just how I felt about myself. If I was in a relationship, as unhealthy as it may have been, I felt whole, loved, secure and validated with a touch of violation all at once.

By the age of 15, I had a son. *My very own child.* One to love and who I vowed would teach how to love me back. I was committed to raising him perfectly. I got a job, finished school, and

I even took the time to educate him, starting with the essential first *ABC's, and 123's.*

My first apartment was at the age of 18 years old. My employ was working in Radio Broadcasting; first as a receptionist and then Marketing. I marketed products and advertisements to other stations for better income. *I loved the experience and the perks.*

In time, I was considered to be a *"Gipsy,"* because I couldn't find contentment in any one location. Even when it came down to my *form* of worship, rather it had been *my living room as* my church, *my bedroom* many times also as my sanctuary, *my kitchen* used as the fellowship hall or the back porch... none of these were stable locations no matter where I tried to take *my praise.*

My grandmothers would tell me to stop running from God and my Parents, (who at the time were not big time church goers) would call me a waste of talent. But because I was in the media, on the air, behind the scenes, and the life of most parties, I didn't feel like I was a waste of *anything.* I constantly heard the statement, *"God put so much more in you, and he's waiting for you to let him release it."*

Raised AME Zion, grew up Pentecostal; could shout better than the best of them and studied every denomination in between. Yet no matter what I studied, God would call my name, and no matter how many times I heard *His* call, I wouldn't stop *doing me* to listen to what He wanted. I even took a five-year hiatus and studied life lessons. Even still, I was blessed with my jobs, was able to produce money, support myself and buy anything else I thought I lacked or even needed. I still had some kind of insight, *so I believed,* and it made my hustles favored, or at least seasonally successful.

Then there was "*the Church thang…*"  During one of those "*I will trust God with all I got,*" stages, there was a church where all the young people in town seemed to attend. I was accustomed to the format. The choir was awesome.  Young ministers were getting ordained. I just knew I would develop this *Church thing* there. Some of my peers had it together at a young age. They understood that voice. *That call from God.*  They were even getting married, preaching, prophesying, laying on of hands (*anointing others*). The preacher was young, and the congregation was filled with folks I knew… went to school with, yet I didn't know how their relationship with God came into play, and I was wise enough not to question it, but I wanted my share.

So one night after I had been in service talking to God, I heard *a still small voice* tell me to go up for prayer. So, I went up, even took my son with me, and for some reason kept him very close to me. When the preacher told me to lift my hands, I obeyed. I wanted to be laid out in the spirit like everyone else at the Alter. I cried out to the Lord, "*This time Lord let it be you…I need you, Lord…I love you, Lord,*" and every other term I was granted to utter.  Then it was my turn.  The preacher was about to lay hands on me, but I was still calling on the Lord.  I desired to feel his touch.  The preacher raised his hand and as he focused on touching me… a force blocked his first attempt.  But, he tried again, this time he asked one of the young ministers to assist him, they pleaded *the blood* over me, they took hold of the oil, yet still, they were not able to touch me. By the third attempt, I held my son even closer, and I felt a quiver all over my body… then a boldness. I left the Alter, got our things and left the church, never to return.

Upon my getting home, I immediately trashed all the weed and liquor in my house. I fell to my knees and asked God to save me. Take this away from me. Answer me! Tell me what just happened. *Am I not a child of yours? And if so… show me!*

Needless to say, that for months, as I committed to worship at home, I saw that that same Pastor was on the news, after moving the church to Atlanta, he was charged with some very serious felonies. It saddened me. Yet I felt a sense of reassurance that the Father does speak to me, if only I stay '*in tune*' as not to misunderstand what He is teaching me.

Everything is not for everyone, yet the word of God clearly states in the Bible, "*Touch not my anointed, and do my Prophets no harm.*"

Still restless in spirit, my heart now longed for answers that the church didn't seem to be able to answer, so at this point in time, I converted to *Islam*. A more practical way to worship. A more disciplined study of religion. A structured way of life; offering my deeds as my way into Heaven. *I went in hard.* My name was still *my name*, but my life consisted of praying five times a day…. covering my head… the Wudu…cleansing my hands, joining a community of believers every Friday for Juma, paying Zakat, fasting during Ramadan, and many more rituals. I even fell in love with a Muslim man, his family, and I let him teach me all about the ways in which he lived. When he moved out of state, I would visit. Loved all the praying, and learning.

Then on one visit, I just so happen to answer the phone and the cheerful voice on the other end, greeted me as if she knew me well. In part I suppose she did, she was the *first* wife and right upon my finding that out, my wonderful surprise, this particular visit, was to be asked to be *the third wife*. Needless to say, I had no idea there were '*any wives*', nonetheless, because I had put the Holy Spirit on the shelf, I couldn't even hear God's warning if I

17

tried. So, with no relationship with the man, I removed my soul from the relationship with the God *I was raised to know and departed from the gifts that I was blessed with at birth (or so I thought)!!*

Here I was… young and naïve'… in yet another dilemma!

# CHAPTER ONE
## All of A Sudden

Just months after renouncing my faith as a Muslim, I tried the streets again. I picked back up smoking, drinking and this time I used sex as a weapon. That is until *Granny* put it out there, "*You have time for everything but God...You better believe He's going to get your attention!*" I had it all put together.... *this was my life.*

Days, hours not even minutes after walking out the house, going to a dart game, ignoring the wise words spoken into my life... I accepted an invite to breakfast, entered a car with three other people, and before I could respond, we were hit by a drunk driver. Not a scratch on anyone else, except for me, a back seat passenger. Til this day I am not sure what my head hit, but it split my skull, in the middle of my forehead, three layers and twenty-three stitches later, I am reminded of it, every time every time I look in the mirror.

While I was under the anesthesia, I was reminded that a child of God will encounter many things, most voluntarily, others because of God's will. This reminder was very convincing. God made it so that only one special Doctor would be available to perform my surgery, and it just happened to be his last night at the hospital. God favored me that night, and from there, I became more aware of *His voice.*

My focus changed after that point. I wanted to make a difference. The desire to be more positive about all walks of my life with family, my one child, friends and more than anything witness about how good God was. The more God blessed me; the closer I wanted to be to Him and the closer I got to Him. Now, I didn't have it all down packed yet. But I was determined to try and get it right. I studied the word but still struggled with the stronghold of fornication.

After having my second child, then third, I finally got married to a man I barely knew, and lo and behold, had yet another child. The God in me would not let the 'Adam' seed die. I believed like the song says "*I made it because I had you (Lord) to hold onto.*"

**All of a sudden**... less than a year later, I was divorced and back at *Granny's*. My constant. My main revolving door. Working at U-Haul and even in the midst of my troubles, still found time to motivate the Community and its Leaders. Attended Church regularly, even when asked to "*Sit down from working in all the ministries.*"

For one year.... I spoke to God.... waited on Him.... while I worshipped. I stood still awaiting his answer on what to do and where to go next.

First, God placed me back in *Radio.* Then he sent me to *Wednesday Power Lunch* at a Baptist Church, then he sent a Pastor to the station to voice a segment called "*Unplugged,*" every weekend. During this time God let me see that life with Him involved using His gifts to uplift the people in the world.

A teacher was put in my face that gave the word that would affect the betterment of the world and was very relatable. My mid-week visit for Bible Study became more frequent which led me to worship a couple times a week. Then came a meeting, with the Pastor, to properly offer membership. I was also asked to join the dance ministry as an Assistant, as the Church prepared to visit Roanoke, VA to render services there.

Meanwhile, God continued to work in me. But really begin to *work on me* was more like it. The job at the Radio station was all about what He could produce, therefore, after an anointed trip, I returned to adhere to God's voice only. By this point, I had lost my grandmothers; all hell was breaking loose with my oldest son, layoffs, underpaid yet working, speaking my truths, asking for God's blessings prior to anything I did. I asked the Pastor if I could "use" the sanctuary before Wednesday service, and with a proud "yes," on my knees I went. In came the Holy Spirit, and out came God's answer into my life.

Upon looking up, I was not alone; this is when I learned what intercessory prayer was, not even realizing how long I had been interceding. Within two weeks, I was back in the Pastor's office, sharing with him how God was preparing for me to move out of State. For the first time, I confided in someone as to why I was carrying so much hurt, hidden behind work, decorated with God's blessings. That Wednesday after Bible study, my Pastor gave a testimony on my behalf, then laid $100.00 at my feet and began to pray over me, for me. The money just flowed from people that only knew me to be a tambourine playing woman, who was always in the newspapers for doing something positive in the Community, or shouting at an old Baptist Church, a dancing, praying, new girl at Calvary.

I had quit my job by then, and they fronted on my last check, but GOD! The money that the Church gave exceeded the amount owed to me, and to make it even better, I had a garage sale that was overly successful. I was even able to produce my famous

*Pastelillios* in abundance, with pre-orders in the amount of five hundred and better!

### Time to Go...

Before I knew it, my day to depart had arrived. My Uncle who helped me pack and plan was ready to drive, and a family friend was ready to put all that was left, into his van and off to Petersburg VA, where God promised me He would develop my calling.

Months passed, family turned on me and my boys, and we were *homeless*. But God kept us. We had a Church to go to... yet, that was ground that was fertilized by my tears, but from them (the group of Ministers and Parishioners) God produced a job, and a house, giving me time and money to adjust to my new surroundings. Did I slide back, *sure did*, and the deeper I slid, the more God took back, piece by piece. But just when "*I*" was about to give up, God stepped in and said "*I didn't bring you this far to leave you, try me... with it all.*"

So, I did. I developed a more intense prayer life. I followed *His* lead... even when I lost my apartment, each step that *He* placed in my path, rather in a dream, or in wisdom, I had no other choice but to *believe*. But the day I truly trusted God, was when I was at my lowest point. I walked into my prayer partners home filled with tears, speaking boldly to *God the Father*, telling Him, that "*I*" couldn't go any further. I needed Him... to feel Him again... to know Him, not just what people saw over me, but *Him* to occupy me. That day, I was bent over praying to God, when *He* took everything that was in me and made me regurgitate *everything that was in me, old, new, real old, real new*, it smelled of burning flesh, it felt of a great release.

For years, I imagined how much more prepared could I be to operate in his anointing with the right teaching, then I read in the word, that God *will give us Pastors of his own heart for us*. Yes, I had experienced some awesome leadership, yet none that just knew. So the Sunday when the Holy Spirit spoke to my children, he told them to direct me to Trinity Missionary Baptist, or better yet, the Daycare Church. Looking *for a miracle, expecting the impossible, seeing the invisible*, I was obedient, I went! Walked in and was *greeted by God, the Holy Spirit. Seeing God the Son all over the faces of the ushers*, I felt comfortable, at home, like God himself *sat me down, wrote the sermon, was the voice of the choir, shared his tambourine, gave me a tissue to wipe my tears, and my answer to invite all visitors* and did it with a boldness.

Then, the Pastor spoke directly to me; he called me out, asking me did I know my calling… the calling of being an *Evangelist*. As I was lead to the Altar… I felt God, He came back, and welcomed me with a warm heat of flames only produced by the Holy Spirit. I recall the Pastor and the Minister's touch. I remember their prayer and confirmation that I am called by God to be what he has called of me… they deemed it to be *Evangelism*.

## A Solar Moment:

To this day, I am committed to learning the word, applying it to my life, preparing to teach it, and continuing to make sure that I am out of the way, so God the Father, God the Son and God the Holy Spirit can manifest Himself in my walk. And, because I am sure that this is where God has placed me, (in the center of His will). I am obedient to God's chosen leader, as to whom much is given, I truly understand that even more is required. Therefore I am walking in my calling with guidance, security, support, love, correction, and first and foremost, the voice of God prevailing in all I do.

# CHAPTER TWO
## State of Mind

I arrived in Petersburg, VA early in the morning. We left Buffalo, NY like runaway slaves, middle of the day... no grand alerts to anyone. *Just locked and loaded*! I'm tired mentally, physically, emotionally, and I really didn't want to talk or cry anymore. But, I can't wait to tell just how funny God can be.

So where do I start... do I share with all of you just how much my heart longed for change. I think my recommendation letter said it best, 'From the desk of the *Boss Lady* herself'... "*She has at 31 years of age, exceeded promotions and sales expectations.*" Or words from my *Pastor*, described me as "*A woman who trusted God undoubtedly until she saw the power of God move on her behalf in a matter of days.*"

From the look of my family, I must have bumped my head, yet, trust is a mean thing, especially when it comes to leaving everything you know and move to... *Petersburg, VA*. But that last night in Buffalo, we partied; we drank and partied some more. Before I knew it, I was waking up to the sound of my Uncle's voice... "*Locked and loaded 'em Babes... we're off to a new life today!*" To be honest, I wasn't ready. I didn't want to face the fact that within thirty days of fasting, praying, having crazy visions, and giving just about my entire house away... today was my last day living in Buffalo, NY.

As a single Mom, you always hope that you're doing the right thing, that the *good Lord* would protect you from the rage of your

25

oldest child, that even your mistakes would find a place of refuge. My oldest son (at that time) created a place in his heart of HATE! Yes... a bitter location that targeted my heart daily. And even upon painting a picture of a new start for him...he connected with the spirit of his living father, one that I fought for so long... until the moment came... for me to realize that he was at an age to know right from wrong. The life of selling drugs, staying out at all times of the night, and the girls, the girls...the girls... not to mention the fact that he was a gifted football player, yet he had a charm about him that could win over anyone willing to be fooled by it.

So, without forcing *Juicy* to join us, I let his choice to stay with his father be just that, on him, by noon we were on the road. I, with a hang-over, my other three young sons with a look of fear and my Uncle with support. Oh... I can't forget the loving couple that decided to let me fill the rest of their Van with the remainder of my things and followed us.

I was too hungover to cry and *saying goodbye* to a whole bunch of other family and friends was not even a comforting thought, let alone, it would have been a task. But what I failed to recall is we were not supposed to leave until that Sunday. So, as we headed down the I-90 on the highway, and the signal of my phone quickly faded, as well as the voices of all my loved ones I called, rushing with boldness, "*I love you,*" and promising, "*I'll contact you when I get there,*" seemed more than sufficient.

We arrived at my Uncle & his wife's house at the break of dawn, and I was more than happy not to be in a car ever again once we arrived. My Uncle had given the navigation system an entirely new name, and let's just say, I've been delivered from that kind of language. The couple that followed in their trusty van seemed as happy as can be; to be on a working vacation, but, when I think about it, the husband always spoke highly of traveling back at *JB's auto shop.* JB was his brother. In that environment, (where I was the Receptionist for some years), every customer that sat in that lobby had a story to share about the open road and everything else in between. And, boy oh boy, the two of them were the masters of shop talk. *Humph!* When I stop and give it some thought now... I probably gave that place a lot to talk about... *always pregnant, always protesting some cause, forever whipping up somethin' on that old grille. And this last stunt, they still talking about that...*

Before I could complete the thought of my last shop conversation pieces, JB and his brother began to share tales to my Uncles about me over an *early shot of wake up...* how I showed up with this tow truck pulling a very beat up van, a 1998 Dodge Caravan at that...

"*Man, if ya'll would have heard my brother, he told Solar she was crazy as hell.*" He told them how I came in weeks prior about this crazy idea to rebuild a car for the radio stations *120 Stop The Violence Campaign.*"

"*Man, she hit us wit that smooth talk she got, and my brother was like, 'what do I get out of this Solar?... Right, and you know ya'll niece, she whipped up some commercial time, TV, and live this with a live that. Before you knew it, she was in our face with that old beat up Van, and about six weeks to have it ready.*"

Yea, that was a power move for even me, I was able to secure a free van, all the body work, and NAPPA was a sure win for all the parts, a tire or two, and some major sponsors to cover the price of the air time. I knew *Boss Lady* was down as long as we made it happen and made budget. That promotion hit my spirit hard, by the end of it... all I could say was REBUILD ME LORD! And the process had begun...

27

The Shop Owners were funny but real, very real, they knew the deal with me. They knew the love I had for their family, especially this brother, a black man doing big business, raising his daughter. How can a queen not love and support that? So, when I needed help to relocate, they saw it as another opportunity to support me and gave me the help that I sorely needed.

By sunrise we all had a taste for some good food, so my Uncle made us a hearty breakfast, or should we call it a brunch. Once everyone was full of food and spirit, we rested. The newlywed couple spent a little time under the big tree in the front yard, had a honeymoon treat and before I could say '*thank you*' again for their time and good will, off they were. A day or so passed and I attempted to check on them... that's when I found out they spent time in the Pocono's! I was happy they took the lover's route and still made it back to Buffalo, NY safe and sound.

Now that Uncle James, on the other hand, had called all his surrounding family, and made arrangements to see them, so he had no time, rhyme or reason to return home so quickly and showed it. That's how I ended up meeting good ole' Uncle Jerry, *Granny's brother*, heck, I hadn't seen him since her funeral. His visits were not without agenda, and the invites with a $20 here and there, though the investments stopped once, he caught wind that I was really the stepchild of Granny's daughter, besides I helped to stop it anyway when I turned down his twisted extensions of incest that sickened me deeply. Blood or no blood, *Granny was Granny*, and every single one of my children were born under her care, one way or the other!

After about 2 weeks or so, once Uncle James finished visiting, eating, and fishing... He was preparing to go home. To be honest, I think he stayed until he saw me get the children in school, register to vote for President Obama, and until the shaking in my voice when I answered the famous question: *"Now you sure you wanna stay?"* had left.

When he prepared to leave, it was like letting go of the last parts of Buffalo. Yet, my pride stepped right in, pushed my chin up and extended my arms for me to hug him, while it helped me stay obedient to God's call for me to stay here, I was without the shield of home.

**A Solar Moment:**

Right now, at this moment, seeing that this energy is beyond me, it breaks the Matrix of today's civilization. My patience comes from movement of everlasting creations. No denomination will set your train of thoughts free. First, they say you must come through me, for I am the Creator of this fictional lifestyle. Still, can't figure out where you are. Then you must not know where you're from. See, I'm hung and for the most part sprung through the natural remaining of life. The struggle is still in motion, a somewhat curved-type devotion and the masses are not ready for what this tool has to offer. Right now, at this very moment, my state of mind is not virtual, but reality and most still can't reach my energy. Can you see?

# CHAPTER THREE

## I'm Here... Now What?

**That's how it went**... I came with familiar faces. I came carrying a confidence that opened doors and tore down walls. Now, thirty days of fasting, praying, listening to the voice of the *Almighty* has me in a barren place. No resources, no familiar faces, just me, three boys and a willingness to seek first the *Kingdom of Heaven*, and the riches, in Petersburg, VA... "*Lord, are you sure you want me here in Petersburg, VA?*"

The funny thing is how the Father will place folks in your path, like *Rev.* a man of God from Roanoke, VA, (the sister church of my one back in Buffalo, that I met during a Revival that my Pastor had had for his Anniversary). We started talking every day, reading the word, some people actually thought I was moving to be closer to him... *WRONG*! He was a prayer partner and a heck of one at that. *Okay, so my intentions were good.*

With so much of my needing my world to become new, I just felt led to try a few new places of worship, especially since my heart's longing goal in life was to live for Christ.... I mean, "*who's isn't in their own way.*"

Now *Church protocol*, on the other hand, was '*a horse of a different color.*' An observation of my *big newfound Church* was where you were primarily greeted by number, rank or position as opposed to a *smaller Church* with enough anointing to peep the power of those who had it and allowed you to haul it into your heart with no problem (for which I first fell in love with later).

So one fine Sunday, the larger group of congregants would not dare hinder the Order of Services to draw new members; where I failed miserably since I was all about missions… to them… I invited a *misfit*. The young lady that invited was not received well. It was deemed she was '*possessed*' and that I had brought a *demon* to Church with me. I'm new in town… I wasn't familiar with '*who was…or who wasn't* socially acceptable' within their *group of believers*! But yet I was asked by what authority did I have by bringing what I thought as "Christians" we were supposed to do, someone of her caliber into the *Sanctuary, (again question mark)*. Now, I'm really scratching my adult head, with my pointed finger, looking upward and sideways. My mouth was just too big or shall I say my light was shining *too-too bright* as I began to even ask *Leadership* how do you express to a person that is in a domestic violence situation *trying* to find a new way of life… that the Church I invited her to *did not* want to help her.

In addition to the reprimand, I was told I wasn't giving enough money when my means of income was 'learned' and that established the fact that I was not at a certain financial level (a status quo if you will). I was brutally interrogated by some of the 'Ole' Bitties,' "*You don't receive Child Support?*"

Oh yes… you better believe a nerve struck, and then the last one, as I was asked to step down from the '*Dance Ministry.*' I stayed humble and retorted, "*I didn't ask to be put on the 'team' in the first place!*" Though, I longed to use my skill as my worshipping ground during a time of being homeless.

Surprisingly, and in what I deemed in haste, I was told, *"NOT TO COME BACK either!"* Wow! When do you become 'not good enough to dwell in the Church house?' I cried inside.

To add insult to injury, I guess I was seen as a *liability* all the way around. Yet it was alright if certain ones were called out to sexual favors, all in the name of *Kingdom work.* I had to take *that one* and as the *good Book* told me, *"If I am not received in a certain place, to shake the dust off my feet and keep moving."*

That would be one of many instances of what some might call today as *"Church hurt."*

I was finally able to get my children into Robert E. Lee. One of the only accredited schools in the Petersburg school district, because as we found that Ettrick wasn't all it was cut up to be just weeks before Christmas break, as a matter of fact, days were still counting down til Thanksgiving when I began to wake up to my surroundings. Each morning I would get up, check my e-mail on my families computer, apply for some jobs, get fully dressed and go out into the world. Most of the time I'd go down to Old Town and sip on coffee with two older white guys who told me stories of the good ol'segregated days, one was an artist, the other an actor. I was surprised to hear so many white southerners excited to have an educated black man running for President. Every day the coffee spot was more explosive than its name…Java Mio! Everyone from the neighboring offices to the surrounding shop customers would come in and see all the coverage about the historic President Obama on the front of every newspaper.

The Day finally arrived to cast our votes, I mean, who can forget the feeling of possibly having the first African American President to date? NO ONE! Yet, the rain that poured down early that morning had a smell of an unidentified freedom. I took my right to vote to heart, as an obligation, a commitment to all the change that I had lived in the past that my future so longed for. The time came for me to head down to Blandford's Old High School in order to share with many a united front for change…*Obama*!

One, of many, was a little old light skinned lady named Mrs. Ellis, beautifully aged, yet you can tell she was still active with a purpose, and everybody knew her! Yes, everyone. She asked me about my coming to Petersburg. I told her I came from Buffalo, she instantly called me *"Snow Bunny,"* and I smiled and moved with the slow rhythm of the line. The more we moved, the more people spoke to her, the more she spoke back, the more she dropped her umbrella, and it seemed to me that they wouldn't stop speaking, so I offered to hold the umbrella for her. By the time we got inside the school, the rain had stopped, and the anticipation from all the great conversation just had me wide awake, and ready to vote. I mean this woman never thought in a million years that we would have an African-American President, and here we all were preparing to welcome *change*. By the time we reached the front of the line, a proud black man had offered Mrs. Ellis a ride to work… Yes… she was a respectable Cook at the Hospital for many years I had discovered, which was where all of her popularity had come from!! So, I gave her back her umbrella and into the electronic voting booths we both went.

That entire day was *awesome*, it seemed as if everyone was on that same level of *"proud."* That day was history in the making. The silence that crossed the winds were powerful, and I was determined not to let anything mess this day up, not even the fact that I needed to pay my car insurance. *Nope, that would not phase me… and why would it?… I didn't have the money anyway.*

After I had picked my boys up from school, we ate dinner as we had fell into the habit of doing all by 6 o'clock p.m. Aunt Judy didn't really let the boys chill as they were accustomed and it was very clear that no dust can fly around... so the boys must be still, no playing in the house, or outdoors, and if you did, bath, bath, bath...

Aunt Judy was set in her ways, and the one way that seemed to click with us was the *herb*, she was up at sunrise, and by the time I got the boys off to school, I was right along with her. *Rev(still a confidant)* was oblivious to what I was doing, *so I thought*, so I never said a word to him whenever we spoke, but I'd wake and smoke, pray and smoke, shower and smoke some more, yet, that habit cost. Sometimes money, sometimes it meant going to find some good smoke in a town I didn't know. But, that's a dedicated smoker if you ask me.

As night fell upon us, we had all we needed to await the news of who would be the next President of the United States. With a sip and some smoke we heard every State's report, and the closer the decision the more excited I was to realize I wasn't in Buffalo anymore, and how many black men I knew in Politics who would be encouraged by this move. Countdown came and went so fast as the News Media announced *Obama,* the winner! So moved by the outcome, I took it upon myself to call every black man I knew back home and tell him how proud I was that they were active in the awareness of change. *Rev.* said I was crazy, but committed to encouraging others, and that was a jewel.

By this time, loneliness started to set in, and it seemed as if most of my time was spent either looking for work, smoking some herb or talking on the phone to a man, a preacher man, one that I only met once... now, how profound can that be for anyone?

However, knowing this attack on my *once* out of control hormones, I found that I changed my conversation with him… it went from Job the 7th Chapter says to… *"when can I see you? How far away are you… See you in a minute!!*

Before I really knew my way around, I would just drive as far as I could and figure out my way back. Many times, I would just travel almost 15 minutes away. Now both of my Uncles, who lived here, were my fathers' brothers and Uncle Charles was really the one I spoke with prior to coming. His house was the familiar comfort from Granny's, traveling up and Auntie had always been Auntie all my life, and I was still her *Pumpkin*!

I believe I found at least four different routes to go over there, and for the first few months, I still got lost. It was something about the area of *"Colonial Whites,"* or *"The Cheektowaga of Virginia."* My buddies down in Old Town said there would be days when *Black people* dared not get caught in Colonial Heights, as a matter of fact, the bridge that connects Petersburg to the racist area is named after MLK today. It's said that he marched across it on his way to Washington, D.C.

With many warnings about the underhandedness of the atmosphere where I was resting my head every night, I choose to ignore the signs, until it was food stamp time, *the third month in a row*. I knew better than to feed and clothe my children! And because I also knew that my *homemade Pastelillos* would sell… I invested in the house and my hustle… Heck, the way my soul flew out of Buffalo, all I left with *was* the profits from my *Pastelillos* and the blessings from my Pastor and the congregation. So I went to work. I was ready to make some moves now, and besides, my Dad sent me a sweet $100.00, there it was, a plan…. A plan to invest, sell, pay and move! That became my number one priority. I needed my own place "by any means *legitimately* necessary."

**A Solar Moment:**

Never would have made it without you, yes you Lord! I'm stronger because I stepped out on faith. All of a sudden, I'm wiser because first I sought your face, Oh God! I'm better because I know that the plan you have for my life is good, all good.

# CHAPTER FOUR

## This Could Change My Testimony

I put my hustle hat on… and off I went with a warmer bag full of my very own creation of flavors in a deep fried shell. I went to every barber shop, auto shop, corner store and greeted every person I encountered along the way. *Kingdom Cuts* was like a *gold mine*. Not only did they fully support my hustle, but it was one brother in there getting a haircut, who, for some reason, (*Will the Barber,* who cut my boys hair for free when the Owners' were not in), told me that this dude'*s*" opinion was like the *Don of food* or something. (Today, he would be like '*Chef Ramsey*'). So, I put on my game face and gave him that shark smile, "*I got just the thing for you… if you can stand a Lil' heat… jerk chicken that is….*"

By then, he must have peeped that I had some game with me, "*A'ite, I'll buy two, and if I like dem joints, I'll get some more from you later, is that cool?*" He sounded so *country*, but a sell was a sell, and all I knew is that they were good. So I gave him 2 for $5 and my phone number!

That day, I not only made the money I needed to pay for my car insurance, but I made a little extra too! And because I cooked them in the house of "*we never fry anything…*" I had to compensate Judy. So back up to *Kingdom Cuts* to ask *Will the Barber* who had some *good green*, and out of all people, he told me, "*G*" the same dude who bought my Pastelillos. What made matters even more hilarious, he came walking all cool around my Honda car. When he leaned down, and I saw that smile, with that fresh cut, that gold tooth, and he smelled good. I was thinking, "*Hmmmm.*" Not to mention I hadn't had close contact with a man since weeks prior to leaving Buffalo. (Yet, in retrospect, I had enough men in my life that, the next one needs to be a permanent fixture for me and my boys).

*G* made sure he told me how much he enjoyed my meat pocket and asked me where I'd been lately. I told him all the places I had introduced to my creation to, and before I could ask about anything else, he found my weak spot...."Do you smoke?" I quickly replied, "Do I? That's what I'm looking for right now actually.

*Will the Barber* was over in the ally enjoying a Newport, looking in the front window being noisy. *G* hopped in my car, with a blunt in his hand. I had never seen one to smoke that was already rolled. So needless to say, I looked apprehensive. But didn't want to look like the cops either, because, in conversation, he sure asked, so I called *Will* over to the car, had him hit the blunt first, then I did, and my goodness, it lifted a great weight, or it was just that *good good...* that's how I felt.

This slick talking Petersburg dude was really trying to figure me out, or something, and before I knew it, he asked me if I had any more meat pockets, "*Pastelillos,*" I said with a goofy smile. "*Ok, whatever they are, I got my grill set up down the street from where you live, and if you would like, I can sell a few more for you.*"

*G* was talking my language, and I needed all I could get in sales, but, before I go back to the house, I need my Aunt Judy *meds*, and *G* was most definitely the man of the hour, '*a one-stop shop*,' I thought to myself.

I rushed back to the house, gave Auntie her *herb*, put the rest of the mix in for about fifty more *Pastelillos* and down the street I went.... To catch up with my new business partner. His grille was the size of a truck, and he put everything on it, whole wings, ribs, steaks, pork chops, *and me* if it was possible. He had a deep fryer plugged up waiting for me and my meat pockets, and every client that came by for their dinner, he found a way to have them buy a *Pastelillo* while they waited for their food. I think *G* got a kick out of sticking the money in my back pocket, and I got one out of the steak he grilled especially for me, plus I was so buzzed, and all I could do was cook, smoke and eat. By nightfall, I even had gas money for the week and a new friend.

As the days passed, *G* became a daily name, one that Aunt Judy loved, because he was a nearby plug, *Rev.*, on the other hand, despised him because, I began hanging out with him, and my Uncle felt he was nothing but trouble. *Pa-ta-a-ha-ha*, to me, he was sent for a purpose, and at the time, I learned a lot from him as well. Like where all the jobs were, where to get a phone, local grocery stores, safe way to get some herb, a person to show me even a little adventurous nightlife, and more than anything, he kept me laughing.

Finally, I landed a job at the Local Cigarette Factory. My cousin and I made our way in together to pull a 12-hour shift of packing, standing, and me, *coughing*. It was funny because, I am not and have never been a night person, yet, we went in at night and got off in the a.m. Talkin' about off...I was off. But, it became funny because G would leave these huge meals at my Uncles doorway. I had told him it wasn't such a good idea if he stopped by

41

because they weren't into knowing the neighbors, none the less, he just wouldn't back down at all. Salmon cakes, fried potatoes, toast, and eggs. I was at a loss for words with this behavior. Plus, I'm working on being the *First Lady* of somebodies Church. I mean, that must have been the reason I was on the phone with Rev. every waking chance I got, so G must be the devil, (at least that was my mind's way of categorizing him), yet my flesh was down for whatever he was presenting.

I had lasted two pay periods before my 12-hour shifts benefits kicked in. I went to Church as much as I could and wanted to go more, but, time was in the way, none the less, when we start making promises to God, He so often allows us to *attempt* to follow through. So I made Him a promise to serve Him more and not just more, but better! *Why did I do that?!?* All that did was increase my temptations. So when *Rev.* (of all people) came to my room to visit, it ended up being a bit more than I could handle, (and being a woman like me; one that needed 'a man that's a man'), *no other tendencies.* That was the beginning of meetings that eventually turned into a hotel room stay *here and there.*

The one visit, in particular, I noticed that he was deeply inquiring about my whereabouts as if he knew the places I went between visits with him and I never paid close attention to how busy I really had become. Until he pointed out that I spend a lot of time at night going to Wal-Mart. I just chucked it up to the fact that when he called, my dear Aunt would tell him that that's where I went or did she tell him that I was out with *G* too, was the question. *And what did it matter?!?* Humpf!

This initial move was supposed to be the big one… the one to test physical attraction that was my plan anyway. So, we got a room, thanks to Aunt Judy's daughter's military discount, we ate

Italian food, I had a glass of wine or two and was ready to attack, when we got back to the room, it was on, I saw his flesh, his plump body. He was round... freckled and not really my taste. I mean I've always liked big buttocks, but this was even more than I had desired. But, I had visions of being saved, and with my sex appeal, he could get whipped into being my Redeemer!

I straddled him, it poked me. I let him go hard. Nothing new to a woman of my nature, you know us, *recovering rape victims...* the ones who never put a value on their bodies. His *pole* was supposed to go in there, and if I think it may benefit my fleshly desire, it could keep going deeper and deeper into my abyss rather I liked it or not. In this case, I fell asleep with a heaviness. I laid next to the *man of the cloth,* and my body caught fire in it. He couldn't even try to hold me... my anointing didn't agree with this sin at all!

The next morning, we went to a Sunday service *together* to pray away the guilt, and then back to my family's house for dinner. I even took him to meet Uncle Charles and Auntie. But, when he departed to return to go *back home*, my soul knew he was not my mate. Then, after the fact, I remembered that this was the Sunday *G* was to go to church with me, at the end of the day, my heart felt convicted, yet I didn't call him to share my feelings.

Days went by, and my disinterest in the *Rev.* upset my family, but I really couldn't get with his ways nor could I or he forget the burning feeling of my skin after intertwining with his. At this time, I felt the need to separate myself from men period, but *G* just would not stop! And my Uncles' dislike for him didn't stop either. He even dug up the history of this Petersburg native. Not to mention, more than a few times when I spoke with Rev., he'd scared me, about a vision he had had of me spending time with *G*.

43

The good ole' Rev. was able to tell me more then I thought he knew and was for the most part on point.

I had become so *wide open* that I started spending more time with G and honestly didn't care at this point. Some nights, I would put the boys to bed and just ride around with him. I never asked where we were going. I just knew that I would be taken care of. I would eat if I was hungry, smoke without fear of retribution and have a drink if I just wanted one. Sometimes, we would just get a hotel room sometimes and chill out. On mornings, after I dropped the boys off, at school, I would immediately go five houses down from where I was staying to have breakfast with this man that *would not* leave me alone no matter how many times I told him I wasn't looking for anything more than *just a friend*.

When I walked in this little white house on Courthouse Road, the pictures on the wall seemed all too familiar... *That woman... I had seen that woman before...* I mean I knew that woman, and she knew me. But outside of my Uncles and their families, I didn't know anyone in Petersburg. When *G*, welcomed me into the kitchen, I was lost... I just stood in the living room asking myself aloud... *Who is she,* as he overheard me. He told me the woman in the picture was his Grandmother, and that this was her home... I was delayed in asking her name, and his answer was a slow....

**Solar Moment:**

We live without thought of where our next ram in the bush comes from. When you venture into new territory be mindful of your environment... See the tangible and the intangible around you.

# CHAPTER FIVE

## In Amazement

*"Granny come here... I want you to meet someone,"* G rushed. As she walked in the living room, something automatically clicked. *Election Day!* This is *"Mrs. Ellis, the same woman that I fell in likeness with on that historical day!!*

*"Snow Bunny?!"*

*"Yes, Mama... Mrs. Ellis, it's me! I didn't know we lived this close, or that he was your Grandchild. Wow!"*

*"Yes... this here boy belongs to me, "Gregory Ellis! And as happy as I am to see you again, I'm off to work."* But she never stops speaking as she got closer and closer to the door to leave... *"Boy, you lucky...It's 'Snow Bunny' you up in here cooking for all this time..."* she giggled.

And by the time *G* prepped his famous salmon cakes, Granny was gone, and we went to the backyard for some wake and bake. It was so peaceful, and I enjoyed his company. Even teased him, *'Gregory hun?!'* After we ate, we laid down to watch TV, went back and forth from sports shows to talk shows, to play hitting... to a kiss, then a kiss that leads to a deeper kiss, to a *close of the door*. The touching... the kissing... the grinding... lead to him caressing my breast, rubbing my body... I was completely honest with him. It was a very vulnerable time, and this wasn't a very smart idea. But he kept on massaging my head, neck, arms, and then, I felt him, he applied the condom, as wet as I had become, he

47

slid into my warmth, and we danced in the bed at *Mrs. Ellis'*...his Grandmother's house.

Later, I returned to my family's house, *in Amazement*, only to be interrogated, *"Why was your car down there... you don't know these people... you been running drugs... did you know that?!?... he's using you and got you using drugs too!"*

*"Now hold up now,"* I shouted. *"I ain't using no drugs... I ain't running no drugs, I'm grown, and I can park my car where I please*!" I called *Rev.* to vent, but all he was concerned with was 'why I chose to hang with a low life,' as if he and my family had done some special investigation on this man's life. Well, later I discovered, that *Rev.* had an old friend from *Special Ops Unit*, to follow me, and found that *G* was making moves, none the less, moves that didn't involve me. *Ole' Rev.*, in turn, was feeding his findings to the family, so they, in turn, gave me the third degree.

By the next disbursement of benefits, Aunt Judy had me go shopping for the house. She needed to borrow a couple hundred dollars for some herb from *G*. Strangely enough, I had a revelation the night before telling me to pack some of our clothes in three bins, and to talk to my boys about *transition*. I had been very *in tune* and favored when it came to the recourses I was able to secure, and one that stood out in my mindset was *CARES*. So, the next morning as the words of my Uncle rolled off his lips, that I had outworn my welcome, I had already taken into consideration that CARES was my option at this time.

The next morning arrived so quickly, I remember it like it was yesterday. The fifth day of December. I took my boys to school, came back to the house and awaited my verdict. My uncle said that he was fearful for the safety of his home and that I was not considerate of that. He couldn't help but add that after numerous warnings, my drug habit, (*which was weed only*) was causing too much friction in his house. And his convoluted reasoning was that the money I spent on weed was really funding my powder habit. Wow, if I didn't know me, I would have thought I was smoking more than weed too, his story was awesome, yet, fake.

When I attempted to tell him that the money I used was really for his wife's habit, and that my habit was nowhere close to hers, and that *G* only comes to his house for her when she calls. But Aunt Judy had my Uncle in the palm of her hand. So, I took my bins, but arranged for her to keep my youngest son until daycare started, she owed me that much, for not telling my Uncle *the truth*.

By this time, I had gained a temporary job working for medical billing. Had maintained a routine with *G* by taking him to *Sam's Club*, to pick up his daily grilling needs, before I then head off to go to work myself. This day was all different, though. When I called *G*, I was in frantic tears, miles away from home and *homeless*. I blamed him... I faulted me... I cried out to God... I hated *Rev.* and my family... '*Who does this to people...*'

I called CARES Shelter and asked if they had space available for me and my three boys. They told me, "*Yes,*" but I would need a Police clearing first. I was devastated to imagine that I would be able to gain clearance since I learned that *Rev.* had me under *Police surveillance*. Yet, I had to create a transitional home for my boys. I bought a pack of cigarettes, for some unknown reason, since I didn't even smoke, walked boldly into the Police station, showed my identification and waited as they ran my name, my plates, my history and *my future*. Thirty minutes went by, and the time I would have usually been at *Sam's* Club with my '*Homeboy G,' there* I was, preparing to serve time as a homeless Mother.

49

I arrived at CARES by 9 o'clock a.m., and I instantly began to shake from head to toe. I'll never forget the ladies on staff that morning. One I will always keep close to heart, *Ms. Grimm.* She was tall, slim, gentle yet, possessed power. She placed her hand on my head, recognized that I was a *chosen child of God*, who was off her *written path* and needed help. She signed me in, gave me the rules, and asked me about my boys and my employment. I told her that I had just gotten them in the daycare across the street, via my Social Services Angel's referral, that I had a job through a temp agency that I was not from VA and didn't have a plan at the moment.

She assured me of two things... One, I was safe and two... I would be fine; reassuring me that before I leave CARES, *God,* would assist me in my next season. With that, I went to work, pulled out a smile, and smoked a Newport on the way so I could get used to the taste. See, my Granny use to say... "*If you ever go to jail, have something all the inmates wanted, so they wouldn't bother you...*" So, CARES to me was a sentence, and with the old testimony I repeated for years, " *I thank the Lord I have never been homeless, and I have never been hungry*" was the 'mental' cell block. And until today, I could no longer say that testimony! I silently cried.

The brighter day came, and it went. I can't say fast, and I won't claim slow. All I know is before I could walk out my job doors good, G was calling me... to assure me that he had dinner for me and my boys and that his first day at the deli went well. My heart dropped, and my eyes were filled with tears. And more than anything, I felt that this was only the beginning of something only God can control.

The days came, went and returned again. Daily, I was confronted with all kind of women. *Eve*, who was "*Johnnie on the spot*," the first night as she helped me get settled with the boys. Her masculine ways were just a bit overpowering, but when she offered to help me carry my bins to my room, heck, what else could I say but, "*Yes!*" Or the homeless lady who came in and off the streets, mainly because it was too cold for her to sleep out there, and well, to test the people of God. Her eyes yielded, "If you were a Christian, then you ought to show some signs" attitude. And she claimed she spoke in tongues, yet it was the many people speaking inside of her head. She shared a room with my boys and I, and her smell was very sickening, a mixture garbage and a bad body odor type of stench. An indescribable smell of funk that has never been heard of and she refused to dependently get clean.

The second night, I spent time convincing my boys that it would get better and that this woman just needed some help getting cleaned up and we needed the Shelter too. So try to plug your noses. The night person, who was a Pastor, helped me talk her into a bath. I was even generous as to give her a sleeping gown. Once she got out the shower, she sat at the kitchen table along with the Pastor, myself, and another young lady. She had one heck of a smile.

The conversation started off just with inquiring if the feeling of being clean was welcomed to her. She shook her head '*yes*' and then said, "*Where are your other things?*" The Pastor, who was on staff, told her that the Shelter would give her extra care in the morning. None of us knew, '*what other things*' she was referring too…. Most likely '*food*,' though (or at least we hoped). From that point on, let's just say the woman, who spoke in other '*tongues*,' (speaking jibberish) began to share with us '*that there were two*

51

*other ladies who were outside and that they were also the ones who had her money.'* Now we knew 'something' was missing right then and there... *Because if you had money... you wouldn't need 'Shelter,' at lease not at CARES.*

At this point, the other woman with us in the kitchen, who normally wore a smiley face, began to ask question in the spirit to *'Miss Cleany'* now and so did I. The deeper we went, the more the lady tried to combat with a force of darkness and started *'talking to herself.'* She yelled, *'leave me alone... I don't want you here.'* And once the tone of the voices changed *back and forth*, that's when the three of us began to pray, and anoint all around... we even sprinkled water. The spirits got angrier, and before we knew it, the Pastor prayed some more... the smiley lady rebuked, and I opened the back door... this way the demons that possessed her body could find a way out of CARES and keep that type of action away from my boys. By the next night, I was changing rooms, in case she returned, and on another occasion, me and my boys were moved to another room altogether, and she, thankfully, left CARES for good.

CARES was an open door for numerous people along with their spirits to enter, establish and leave, or fail to plan and wind up returning back because of lack of a plan. There were the Battered Mothers, who were running from their relationship, the pregnant teens who didn't want to listen to their parents, folks who claimed they were affected by the recession and then there were the ones who came, told their story, and was gone. The women I met in CARES cried like me, ate like me and provided for their children like me. Regardless of how many sleepless nights I encountered... I got up every morning, dropped the boys off at daycare, picked G up, went to SAM'S Club and by 9:30 a.m... off to work I went.

Now, the one thing that came in super handy, (especially with me trying to save money to leave CARES soon), was the fact that the Shelter would send me to work with enough lunch food, that I could feed my entire department. One of the Supervisors saw it and showed favor upon me.

Chores changed nightly at CARES, the staff rotated, and all the women did what they had to do to get by. So between going to Church in Prince George and back to the Shelter, I held a Bible study with the ladies from my New International (Relationship) Version (*NIV*) of the Bible. Other than that, I stayed to myself and attended to my boys. I avoided drama while I was there and the closest I came to it... was when someone's laptop got stolen, and at four a.m., all the women had to get up so that everyone's room could be checked. My roommate was the victim. When the police left, I confronted the thieves, the victim, and the staff, because we were all a part of this four a.m. crazy situation. *But stealing? I was livid.* I had work... my boys had school. *This must be a dream*!

**A Solar Moment:**

 With eyes shut, I look from behind closed lids. I am determined to keep my eyes open, so I can see what lies ahead. Using MY experiences, afforded me the eye opener that I needed so I could get by and get on with my life.  My children are the most important thing to me, and I hope you would agree that before it could ever be destroyed, you too, will go miles high. I will never give up. I will never let go.  My eyes are on the prize of a higher calling.

# CHAPTER SIX

## Starting Over

Well as my life in Petersburg, VA played forward, so did my issues that totally stripped me. I saved up enough money to leave the Shelter and move into my first apartment, yet that was as life changing as anything I had ever experienced.

I did a lot of thinking while in that low and crazy place of extended shelter, *40 days and 40 nights, how ironic*! No permanent job yet; but a commitment to pay rent and the closer I walked to those exit doors, the closer I was to seeing other doors opening...

Like the Catering job, *G* and I landed, from the Supervisor of my temp job and my girl *Gi-Gi*, who always had my back, she lived in Hopewell, by way of NYC. Along with so many others, like *Freddie* and *Will the Barber.* Oh yes, by the time I reached the door, with my boys in tow, I felt the tears welling up but refused to let them fall

My eight months in my new apartment on Wilcox Avenue was spent blessed and cursed alike. Blessed because I moved in items well collected in a narrow storage space, two cars and three trips later and I was good to go! No beds yet; but hey, that lasted about a week or two. When I looked up; it was fully furnished. And if you can't take my word for it, ask my neighbor, Ms. Candy. By the walls not being completely up, she saw the rapid progress. Yes, I said... *no wall* to completely separate us during the renovation of this apartment (but I took it)… which lead to G thankfully staying the nights and most days because of it.

It was a strong agreement prior to this living arrangement presented to G….that we could not, would not can not *"live"* together. But, one comfort lead to another and sometime within that eight months, he had a stroke, and my house served as a *House of Refuge* to an unforeseen amount of unknown *"friends of his"* as I ran the catering business. I continued working and when I wasn't collecting unemployment (*when you still got an actual check*) to keep the bills paid, and the house afloat, our selling food sustained me and my boys. *Good thing the rent included the utilities.*

I also frequented the Prince George place of worship and continued the dance ministry. I enjoyed it to the fullest; no… not being the sole provider…. *Dancing for the Lord; "It's what I do!* My flags were my *safety nets* and weapons to ward off spirits and ammunition to put on *the whole armor*. The green flag represented *prosperity and wealth*, the white, purity, the purple, *royalty*, pink, *healing* and gold *holiness*. And I waved them while dancing and praising the Lord in Church with all my might too, *Jack!*

When G's health was restored, there were nights, I would fall asleep on the couch hoping he would come through. Especially, the one night… I had a birthday party, but he went elsewhere. *I was tight!* Yet, I kept telling myself, that the *Yolanda Adams* song about her *then* husband, who was her *old pusher, gone saved man,* was written just for me. Yes, I believed *that if I could just stick in there,* she says in the song, that she was his *'El Shaddai,'* the *angel, sent to save his life. Yet the white lines kept him away from seeing all of me. More than anything he couldn't see his self.* We had a routine of tolerance, even when the house got robbed, we maintained a sense of, *"we got each other back."* My first real

*Bonnie and Clyde* relationship. *"Oh, what I fool I was,"* thinking I could save anyone when *it is* and *always will be* that of the *Lord's doing.*

*Yikes,* a lot happened within the first eight months… My parents decided to visit, and I was grateful that I had actually completed something. I had my CPA certification (even if it was required to keep my benefits). But it was important to me that they saw me *"accomplished."* Outwardly, anyway! Inwardly, I was battling… not to mention bills in the house were going up, back taxes, folks starting shooting at the neighbors… *The walls were up by then… Thank God*! And I had yet to figure out where *G* and I were headed…

Jazz Festival #1 was a hit… then it was time for us to go to Richmond, VA selling our food. We made the menu, we seasoned the chicken… weeks of prep, and then the week before the event, I drove my boys to Buffalo for the first time since we left. On the way back, the tire flew off my car, but five hours and one day later, I arrived at my home to be greeted by G, lavished with flowers and a great steak dinner… *"Ah, vacation… two weeks… no children… what will I do?"*

Towards the end of my *"starting over,"* season… I also took a week-long job at a woman's house who was deaf. By day four of the job, I received a call that my house was being raided, and they saw me serving an informant….*"ARE YOU KIDDING ME?!… HOW?… SERVING WHAT*?!" Well, that boiled down to… *"they found some weed and powder in my apartment and G's I.D…* "

In my *DMX* voice from the movie *'Belly'… Impossible to go home*! Can't afford to call off. Have to stay *24/7* at this ladies house until the "coast was clear." A blessing in disguise, all I could do was perform *sign language* to the best of my ability. Grateful for it during the stay, actually. Whew.

G was not answering his phone, and he has my *Honda*. I'm pee'd! When we finally reached one another, the first thing comes to mind is… 'what *heifer* he got selling from my car while I'm here bussin' my butt off?!' but the first thing I could muster up to actually come out of my mouth instead was…. *"Bring me my doggone Honda*! My constant…. Me and my *Honda* was inseparable.

Needless to say, G was on the run (yes I got a fugitive on my hand), to say the least. The entire ordeal was a bit much, and that Saturday morning couldn't have come fast enough. I rushed to my ruined apartment… it was all messed up!! The cops got me looking at G so crazy. I was scared to go back home… to my own place… *to live there anyway*… let alone bring my boys back there. I can't focus. G's all messed up mentally. Yet, we both were told that after careful review of *the warrant* it was possible that they had gone into the wrong apartment! *"ARE YOU SERIOUS?!"* And that they were sure that the information they found *still* had no business in my home, especially with children. *"Favor."* Now, I really needed a place to go, with no prospective spots in sight, until that night when I went to the *little lady's house* who I met in the voting line, my friend, *scared and shaking*! She probably thought I was *an addict*. But with loving kindness, she ran me a shower, gave me a stiff shot, and put me in her bed, where she rocked me to sleep, soothing my fears. *"Think about tomorrow, tomorrow child, God knows, he has a ram in the bush, now go on to sleep, you safe here and that boy of mine knows to stay where he at. Now, you just rest."*

*"Thank you, Mrs. Ellis, you are so comforting,"* even though I felt like *"Bonita in Wonderland,"* somebody… but I smiled myself to sleep.

One year later, I was still very active in full-time Evangelistic Ministry, this time at a C.O.G.I.C affiliation had a career change and became the Day Care (where my boys attended), Administrator. Did I mention, *"I love the youth!"*

G even came around to understanding me a little bit better. Full time loving my sons and part time loving me. My decision, in part… I needed a *"Soulmate."* So he knowing how important *Evangelism* meant to me, ended up even getting baptized. He often referred to me as being too, *"Intense."*

But it just happened to be my level of sincerity when it came down to *the things of the Lord.* Besides, Granny warned me… *"Never to play with God, and how it was a terrible thing to fall into the hands of an angry God."*

So, I still continued to do what I did best and stayed actively involved in various other Ministries of the Church besides dancing, speaking and witnessing. I produced results for Cooking Ministry, Fundraising, Revivals, and Concerts, as well as weekly Sisterhood breakfasts'. Although I was still carrying some heavy bags, *and they were heavy,* instead of *giving the load* to God like *He* said, (in primarily taking care of my family singlehandedly), I didn't leave my *Church work* behind, though. I even went shopping with the Sisters and Mothers, went on retreats, planned trips, learned valuable life lessons from the *aged ones* and actually thought I was close with the younger women of my age group, since we even *broke bread together* – 'boy was I wrong.'

When jealousies crept in; it was like I entered a whole 'nother dimension, *in the spirit realm.* The faithful Mothers of the congregation prayed for me as I told them about how important it was for me to *fast* and how I wasn't being received well. *'To put it mildly, I could have stayed outside the four walls for what I was encountering inside.* One thing I noticed too was that the more involved I became in Church and others in it, the further I got away from that *G too.* I needed more, and a new living assignment was about to take place. As it is traditionally spoken, *"battles within, fears without."* There were pulpit battles, member battles... I couldn't fathom someone dogging the *Pastor*, but many disliked me for not joining their bandwagon. *How could I?* I didn't know what their agenda was... I had one purpose and one purpose only, *'to edify.'* Seemed like the more I served, the harder it got. My attackers had a face *with a smile on it.*

Well, me and my mouth... *yep, that thing...* I snapped, one day, because confusion didn't belong in the *House of God...* and let it be known that I was not pleased with how things can go for so long or get covered up more than once, but it was time to *'put some stuff on the table!'* *Did anyone learn anything from my full six weeks course on "Self-Discipline class?*

I must say, this particular Sunday, after service, I was approached by a *Sister* and her family. They were headed right in my direction to come *jump me.* I saw it afar off and asked my babysitter to hurry and get my boys home, they don't need to see this. I was determined to stand my ground, even if my VA family didn't have my back. They were just standing around looking dumbfounded. I didn't know how to *"turn the other cheek."*

**A Solar Moment**:

Some things I left at the door before going inside to the Altar.
Know your assignment and how long it takes to complete it.
Prepare for the task ahead. Otherwise, you will be operating in the
wrong season. You will be in *Fall*, thinking it's still *Summer*, when
you should have removed yourself from the issue last *Spring*.
Don't ignore warnings when the *Season* is up.

# CHAPTER SEVEN

## Surrender

*See... what had happened was...* It was requested of me to coordinate a Youth Revival, called "*Fall Back Haters.*"And though I was perfect for the assignment since I had taught the six week '*Self Discipline*' course, not everyone saw '*eye-to-eye,*' and I walked away from the fight with a *black eye* from being jumped. Needless to say, the title for the *Revival* fit the bill. *But I was through then*!! I excused the *holy ghost* and started pouncing right back. All the long, quoting in my head, "*fight the good fight of faith!*" Was it silly of me to fight back, "*Yes.*" Was I going to stand there and let someone beat my tail, in front of my sons, "*NO!*" Would I do it all over again, if I had to, "*Yes.*" Do I ever want to, "*No!*" I didn't even know this young lady and her family. Thank goodness, "*YouTube,*" was non-existent back then.

But, boy oh boy, I am here to tell you, just like the *good book* says, "*what's done in the dark shall come to the light!*" These people were *hypocrites!* They were beginning to remind me of *Rev's* church. I was confronted with, "*How... you as an Evangelist.... and cussin' like that and call someone a 'B#&*@.?!'*

"*The same way someone would have the audacity to want to fight in the Church house,*" I humbly responded. Regardless of how any of the people of that Church felt, *I was* serious about one of my favorite songs, "*I surrender all!*"

My punishment, from the Pastor, even though I did not initiate the scuffle, was to "*sit down*" in Church terms. No active participating on any auxiliaries for *30* days (in a child's world today that would be called, *"time-out"*). But that month, I praised God like I was *stupid*.

I was still *'out with G'*.... especially since now he and I weren't getting married, and I had no *ring* in sight. Ministry and shacking don't match *ever*, (*or it will match when that fire light it to my tail and that gets thrown into the Lake*). Oh, I was his *'Angel'* alright. *Which one... was the question*! He also knew I wasn't leaving my *Ministry* and that by now I had had it *up to here* being sick and tired of running from *my calling*, no matter who didn't like me. *Enough!* I already had three little men to care for and a fourth back home, *my oldest*, that I missed with all my heart. They need me, and I need them. *Bye Gregory Ellis*! I must surrender to *His* will.

Far be it, was that day, I will never forget... my holiness almost went out of the window with that frivolous incident. In my defense, nobody saw me laid out... Prostrate... praying for hours and fasting for days... no one knew my struggles. The lonely nights of anxiety wondering if the next day would manifest into something different... how I had to hustle to feed my children.... the men that I had been delivered from... dead weight... compared to the ones that for some reason, who never wanted to leave, all in the name of *'lust.'* *From the pimp to the pulpit*, that was a book right there, I thought to write it one day. Yet, people saw my strength, and some even encouraged my growth and creativity, until they find out that I wouldn't compromise with my *faith*.

Over the next few months, so much had changed in me, and by the time the young lady came back to the church, herself and apologized, I was back on Altar Call duty, Praise & Worship, teaching dance... I had no room to harbor hate... I was not in the wrong and learned early on that *'that my gifts and calling of God were without repentance.'* It was all about surrendering myself to the *King...* It was all about the kingdom.

Before I knew it, it was *Easter* season, time for *'complicated traditions'* and for some reason or another, since I've been in VA, my family had never missed a gathering together, along with dinner. So, my Uncle and his family, and oddly enough *G* and his *Granny, my dearest Mrs. Ellis* were together. We ended up cooking and sharing this *tradition* with our families. By Thanksgiving, I made travel plans, for my boys, myself and guess who wanted to come along... Yes, G! During the trip, the conversation was more serious than ever... as our family mentor the *good Dr. H* would say, *"there has been some growth through all the bull....*hun?"

We actually talked about moving to Buffalo. I mean, both my Mother's had dreams about living back in Buffalo, yet, of course, I questioned everybody first, *but God,* if I should return. For some reason, it consumed my thoughts though and even came from revival messages, billboards, *you name it*! Even revelation came by way of a *Prophetess,* I knew very well, by the name of *Lady Gloria.* She spoke things to me that were just phenomenal. Like myself, she was always moved by the *unction* of the spirit and never let anything get in her way either. She just so happened to be in town for a funeral, right across the street from my house, that I had to attend as well, to pay my respects to a close friend, and once she saw me there... she just began to speak to my heart. She was not new to relocating herself. A proud *'Army Wife,'* she was. And when the two of us, who considered ourselves, as *'the remnant,'* got together, I tell you, we would put those demons in their place!

*Lady Gloria* accompanied me in a Praise Dance equipped with my flags, and it was out of this world! The manifestation of the power of God moved throughout the entire *Wake ceremony*. We left there with family and friends and went out to go and get something to eat, and I could still feel the anointing. I knew right then and there that I had some more moves to make. And even though I was promoted to Director of the Day Care, I would still need to resign. It was quite troubling to me that I had not had a MIT class since I took the position, and to keep it 100% the Board was too deep into *my* personal business. Not to mention, the *Church* I was still at was floating in greed and its watering well filled with lust. Everything *but* the anointing was going on in the confines of the *Sanctuary*, and that troubled me deeply, and as the song says, *"My soul just couldn't rest contented..."*

**A Solar Moment:**

Sometimes you have to *move* to see *the move* of God in your life. Consider the possibility of never transitioning. Then what would be your chance of meeting your Maker? Remind yourself to listen to that still small voice within. When it's time to go…. It's time to go!

# CHAPTER EIGHT
## All Packed and
## Moving Back

With the roaches packing their nest for the winter, and my birthday soon to approach, I felt a spontaneous jolt of energy one Sunday after we danced. Something took hold of me and spun me around and around, the organist just played and the guitar 'was-just-a strumming,' after the message from the book of Exodus, being taught that... it definitely meant someone was leaving. AMEN! The Pastor proclaimed "*it wasn't time... that I would fail if I left now because I was living off $1,100 per month, and I didn't have to pay daycare fee's and I was doing all this for the Church right*?"

I snapped. *Yes, it was time*! So from December to February, I was in reverse. I packed my house, I planned with G and considering the fact that the hopes of him staying behind seemed thin to none, especially since he had been the only man in my boy's life for three consecutive years, come *hell or high waters, I was going back home...*

For six months or so, I considered the offer from my friends of getting me a public housing apartment to start off, while backing that plan up with talks with *Mom Dukes*. Even spoke with *Boss Lady* month's in advance, and she was working without a *Promotions Director* at the Radio Station. I loved this lady, *Mrs.*

*Brown.* I knew her since childhood, seemed like no one else in Buffalo knew her under the same magnitude as I. I am so privileged. As much as she was successful and reserved, she was quiet and stayed incognito. But in the background, she was *the Owner... yes, the actual Owner* of one of the major radio stations in Buffalo and most of the community never knew. *Good news travels slow!* She was one of the brightest, most sincere and intelligent person that I knew. And if she could do something for you, she would, and if she couldn't, she'd find another way to make what *you* wanted to do possible. The question I didn't ask, upon negotiating the job planning, was Lord, how much of it can I jump back into. For some reason, I felt torn. Between radio broadcasting or community liaison. There were so many items on my plate, not to mention a huge community Black History Stage Play, a possible wedding and *another* new church affiliation.

Once again, I ignored all warnings, all wisdom, and trust that whatever the plan that I came up with... would be one I would just have to live with but *time* tells all and flew by very fast. I dare not return home without a covering (in the form of a husband), so I went full throttle on wedding plans. *G* understood my strengths and my weaknesses, and I his. He was my second *Rock. Christ* being the first. We failed at some things, G and I and we conquered some things as well. I had to conquer my own *strongholds* though and for lack of patience kept picking them back up for one reason or another. He tried so hard, in a loving way, to protect and encourage me along the way. Even though, we were from *two different sides of the tracks.*

I tried to prepare him for the different *me* in Buffalo than who I was in VA... in Buffalo, I am named *Solar,* and I am looked up to as the *helper* not the *helped.* I explained to my fiancé' what you saw me do in his hometown... That he never encountered what I was about to do at *home*. At home, I was *somebody*! He met me a low state in VA. My job is very demanding, and my Church there... well... put it this way... I laid it all out for him.

And as my actions were of packing and incorporating him, one night he stopped me, in my thoughts with movements, and said, "*I love you, Lady Ingram,* in his country voice... he continued, *and you crazy as hell, and I know I haven't been the easiest going dude,* (trying not to *cuss*), *but I love you and those boys...* He continued, "*And, to be honest until I met you, I never wanted to get married. I saw you hustle in a City with three boys and you kept your head up and you cute, dress real fine but, for real, I rock with you because of who you are, and how you get down, I mean you can go anywhere and do anything you want in life... and I want to show you the support and love I have had for you since day one, you are my friend and my love, and I want you to be my lover for life*". So just like the black history play I had just written and added to my VA collection of play productions, and stage appearances, I planned a small backyard wedding, and a departure plan thereafter.

*Orange, yes, the colors orange and brown* came into my spirit, and my dress was perfect for me. The more I planned to leave, the more the Pastor tried to put more on my plate, even to the point of asking me to leave without saying *goodbye* to the congregation. I could see if I was asking them for gifts or something. But I kept it moving anyway, and so did G. We decided not to have that particular Pastor marry us at all! Instead, our choice was my hairdresser, who was an Ordained Minister to perform our nuptials and it was her husband who helped *G* with his tux ensemble. I always looked up to them as a prosperous couple, when I first met them anyhow. So far as I was concerned, I had my boys, and we had this great couple by our side. I was *good!*

My hairdresser and her husband had a barber shop with the beauty shop upstairs, and they did their thing in the community, without all of the fanfare that goes on inside the *church walls.* I even danced *for free* every year at their *5ᵗʰ Ward Reunion.* And by the time G and I was ready to say *"I Do,"* this awesome Minister and husband kindly offered to cater the reception. G was excited about his chance to change his life, and we had a plan... and we were going to work it!

I knew one thing, for sure, though and that was that I desperately needed to take a trip alone before going down the aisle again. So, I decided to take a train to go spend some time with *Prophetess Gail,* my *Army wife* friend, along with her husband of thirteen years to clear my head and get some words of wisdom. *Good thing...* because when I returned, after just one week, back to VA, I noticed that G had barely packed. He didn't want to talk about the wedding at all and when I asked *was he scared,* his answer was undoubtedly, *"Yes!"* Then followed with a... *"I really think we should wait until we get to Buffalo to say I do!"* When I asked him, *"Why?"* He confessed that he was afraid that I would *put him out.* But, my charm, coupled with my persuasion, talked him into marrying a woman *not fully healed,* for the sake of security.

The countdown was slow but fast at the *same time.* The more I packed to say goodbye... the more stuff I seemed to have. The more I wanted to get married.... the more reservations set in. And then when my Father called to ask me once again *"to wait"*... That was all it took.

**A Solar Moment:**

To everything, there is a season and a time for every purpose under the Heaven. Ecclesiastes 3:1

# CHAPTER NINE
## There's No Place Like Home

Lucky for us, the Honda was ready to make the trip, after much-needed repair. No paint job, but, hey, she was fixed. Job position was secure. I would be able to start April 1st. Now, all I had to do was get through the next two weeks. I was finished with the assignment at the Day Care, and no matter how much I got done in my three room apartment, it seemed there was always more to be completed. It didn't help that *G* always found a way to have me or the boys busily at work with the business. But I felt like a Queen there, well most of the time, until the *unfamiliar, familiar folks* would stop by the restaurant to not only grab food but *Meds* (I had grown accustomed to calling the transactions). We had moved too, by the way, to the historical district in Petersburg. Very rich history was in this particular vicinity too. And as much as I felt like I belonged, the more I thought that there was '*no place like home*,' and all I could think about was my return. So we packed and packed the U-Haul truck.

I was so excited to get a call from one of my old producers... Strangely, a friend had passed away from one of my first poetry groups, and my presence had been requested for *Spoken Word* for the last *Wordism by Love London,* and the event would take place one week after my arrival. My itinerary was already filling up and without a doubt, my coming back to Buffalo, NY was needful.

When we arrived, it was *cold* outside... that good ole' Buffalo snow and dark clouds were the warmest welcome one could expect

75

when coming into the area! We took our bags inside my parents' house and all of a sudden, I felt a sense of comfort, a desire to truly relax. Yet, the hustle of getting all my boys in school... unpacking and then adjusting, along with my now 34th birthday, fastly approaching, I had not even given a second thought to my "*Man.*"

From day one, because he was not comfortable or raised in a home like mine... We had disagreements before I knew it, I had secured a temporary job to have some of my *own* money flowing until I started my permanent job at the radio station.

Each morning, I would get up for one week straight, all alone at 3:30 a.m., go into my prayer closet, prepare myself for the day. The cold, the responsibilities of *just life*, get breakfast prepared, pray about non-prejudice schools for my sons and what Church I would be led *to attend* and contemplate on the way to show *G* how to maneuver in a *strange land* and how to get the catering business re-established. Finally, I prayed for strength that everything would work out. This was home, and I was here to stay! And *G* stayed at my brother's, since after selling dinners it was quite late anyway, (and besides he wanted to stay out of the eyesight of my Father, who was still, very protective over me) and although my brother was brilliant... had a great mind... he was also into the *streets*.

Now, that opened up a can of worms.... because once *G* began to ask me for financial help, I began to worry. We were already running low on savings, I was paying the little bit of bills we did have, and well, between smoking, and drinking, and a few haircuts here and there, I am not sure what else *his* money was spent on. So I just chalked it up as he wasn't really making much money. Eventually, when I began my real position at the radio station, my time got scarce, and I began to see that two jobs were really for *two* people, so I gave the temp one up. *G would have to pull his own weight.*

Easier said than done, we had now begun to argue about any and everything, from my parents to jobs, to money, to his ongoing lies… about the smallest of things even. He would get so high sometimes (off of some herb), get the munchies and eat up all the food that *I* purchased for my boys primarily. So even that welcomed a new argument. *"Eat at my brother's… don't be coming over here eating us out of house and home… This my parents' house too, you know… and find us a place… you have more time on your hands than I do!"*

As Spring swiftly approached, and winter departed, my hours were becoming very intense. Let's just say the more I was away from home, the more we found words for one another. Then my Mother and Father began to question our living arrangements because Granny would say, (with all of her sayings), *"Houseguest and fish stink after three days…"* And my parents had the gift of discernment, and they were going in… they never *minded* asking *any* questions, *"Well, is he looking for work… or is he just sitting around all day at yo' brothers' house… did ya'll find anything yet?"* and the like. *And…* they could see my future better than *Cleo.*

The shocker came after my visiting Church with my parents, a few times, and the when the Pastor was able to see past my silent sittings, and tell me about my calling, knowing that I had not been under the proper ministry and training, and how I need to share the *gospel* with my new husband.

In turn, *G* came to Church the following Sunday and joined, pulling me and taking the boys down the aisle with him. (*How embarrassing this moment was, yet, I followed*). The dangerous part is he knew that I had a passion for working in ministry. This was a very large ministry, nothing like the one I came from under back in VA, which meant there was more of a demand on real people of interest and, well, I called myself trying to slow walk it, especially since my time at work was so hectic. But, I felt the tug and the need to be involved, (*why just sit on a pew and take up space*). I feel everybody in the Church should have or be given something to do. So here I was being encouraged by the man I love, "*Do you, baby, you the Evangelist, you helping to save me, I don't want to mess with what you gotta do.*"

Like any newlywed couple, we were looking to make the best of *starting over*. We even accepted the offer to move into this older house, upstairs from my sister and her family, in the house that our Granny had left, and it's funny, I consider this property to be my revolving door, so how comforting it was, for me and my boys.

As far as the man I married, new member or not, there were still some kinks that I surely found out that were not worked out. Like *womanizers* back in VA trying to coerce him into returning and he wouldn't hesitate to tell them, especially if I was within, ear shot, "*We'll see.*" Those conversations would mess me all up. Yet, I held it in... instead of tripping totally... I was still in the process of the '*getting settled*' fog.

It had now been three months since returning to Buffalo, and I was in my own house finally....praying.... hoping that the atmosphere would be at least a bit better now. At times, *G* had seemed to lose respect for my parents and wouldn' t take his shoes off at the door.... A big '*no-no,*' as well as many other, *diss'* and if our arguments weren't grounds for divorce, that certainly *was*.

**A Solar Moment:**

Why is that we look for validation for the most important things in life? Why does doing what you love to do push and pull you at the same time? Is it because what you are really called to do to try so hard not to?.... is it what is most natural... Have you come to the realization that where He leads... He feeds... and where He guides... He provides...

# CHAPTER TEN

## The Day That Took Me Away From Wonderland

*G* continued on with the two jobs, and I kept pushing to break promotional sale records at the station. As festival season came, and the planning for the *50th Hall of Fame* Party plans continued, my time at home was very scarce. And when I was there, my mind, body, and soul would be out of it. Yet, we still had to get settled in our new abode.

Upon arriving to retrieve our belongings from storage, we were greeted by mice! They ate through bins, beds, dressers, toys, t.v's and when I was told nothing could be done... I was furious. I called the Corporate office every day, wrote letters to the newspapers, dignitaries, you name it. Shortly thereafter, I'd receive a response in the form of a truck that pulled up to my house filled with all size mattresses, furniture, and other necessary furnishings. We had been *blessed*. Not to mention, it would have been a grave setback, because we already had our hands full with home repairs, and it took money to do that. Good thing we *both* were working, by now anyway!

Also, by now, two of my sons were able to rekindle a relationship with their biological fathers, though they were dependable, it often brewed resentment for my current well-being since they spoke the language of arguing, just because, I was happy. So, I had to always maintain a level of sobriety since I didn't want any upheavals to come into my home. I had worked too hard and I would probably at this point, in my life… (if I didn't stay prayed up), would have regretted what I may have done to any one of my children's father. But shuddered at the thought of after all I put my sons through, that they would have to ever come see their Mother sitting inside some penitentiary so I would have to handle the situation tactfully.

The boys knew they were loved but were in awkward situations at times. I had yet to reunite my youngest son with his father, who was *MIA*.

But we ate every day. My boys slept comfortably at night, and when it was time to move rather it was from the radio station to pursue other dreams or to a better living arrangement, as the song says… *the Lord will make a way somehow*… And He did. I just had to wake up and recognize *the calling*.

Now, before I pretend as if the home front was all that most thought it was cracked up to be…it wasn't. As a matter of fact, it was filled with uncertain conversations, words that could not be taken back, and influences that made more of an impact than the Savior himself. I was so accustomed to having men in my life that said one thing, did one thing and then asked me to do another. Yet, G and I had a plan, we sat nights on end before moving here and said what we wanted and needed from one another and from Buffalo!

Still, in the midst of all the changes, I fell victim to several familiar pitfalls: my mouth, yes, indeedy! I spoke about everything I hated in the man I fought to marry… it was as if all the plans went out the door. The Government job he took, lasted for a few months and when it ended, it was all on me as it had been many times before. But I thought we had outgrown that. Besides, this was not the first time... I wasn't feeling my job anymore, I was missing my boys and tired of working long hours and new my reign was coming to a swift end... I needed a change, even if it was for a season. Heck, I hustled at my job just like he did... so when was *his money... his money*! *Mine was never mine.* And his hustle with the catering business was *both* of ours... Half of the start-up monies came because of prominent people I knew!

If he had two jobs and I didn't want to work my *one...* then that should have been that... I was tired and had worked long enough. I was working since I had my first son, at the age of 15!! *I been there... done that... why should I struggle like I was a single woman when I was married.* G knew I came with a package deal when we said we would make a go of it... and whatever happened to... "*Lady Ingram, I love you, I adore you, I love them boys, you saved my life!*" So yes, I was in Wonderland, but I'm out now because I had been shelling out so much from my end, trying to make them meet.

It got to the point where I just got angry, yes just downright mad. I felt as if I was doing all the man stuff in our relationship. And to make matters worse, the folks I shared my sentiments with, also felt the same way but encouraged me to rethink my choices in the future, if we should split.

Now the danger in me entering into discouragement with my now third husband, even though one didn't count... *yes... that one... with the multiple wives...* is that it can be very damaging to my sons... and when they start telling you that they don't like where this is headed... you know, the fairytale is over.

The more I fought for the marriage, the more *G* bucked against it... until one day, I said *'fine and well... because my son is not happy with you being in our lives so you can just get the hell out of it!*" My sons were very young and meant the world to me, and I had to protect them at all cost. They will not grow up to see their mother struggle; be bitter and angry and knowing that I had *help*, but that their step-Dad no longer wanted *to help*. They were, at this point and time, getting older and I had four "*sons*," and as far as I was concerned those were all the *men* that I needed in my life.

So I began to wear a mask, a *loving* mask, no less, I did wear and truly was aware of it, *for the most part*. As a matter of fact, I had been wearing this mask for such a very long time, that every time I thought about taking it off, I was afraid. "*Was I wearing the mask or the mask was wearing me?*" One thing for sure, it was wearing me thin, and I had to snap out of it before I would regret hurting someone one else who would not deserve my wrath. My mind wondered, '*Was this God's way of testing me to see if I had what it took to endure. Not just with my children, not just with a Church, but with what he deemed Holy and Sacred. I believed in marriage so why was mine crumbling apart? I had to question that. G hadn't done a whole lot of wrong... was it fair to him, I didn't want a divorce... couldn't we work it out?*'

**A Solar Moment:**

A suppressed feeling can hurt so bad. Somehow, I gave in and thought I could just stop the pain. When someone takes advantage of innocent love wrongfully, silence speaks so loud. Listen to your inner man. I did. I stopped overlooking the proof and started to do me. It still hurts because you want to look back and know that you cannot... not for one iota. *"Remember Lot's wife!"* Even if you're left alone, don't lie about love to avoid getting hurt... it's not love... if it hurts.

# CHAPTER ELEVEN
## What I Forgot To Tell You

*Happy Anniversary...* One year later, I was still complaining and being miserable because I felt I got married against God's will. Perhaps, we needed counseling or I needed a *life coach*. Whatever the case may be, I had better get it together and get it together fast.... My husband was kind, he took care of me and my boys, he provided for us, he made me laugh even when I wanted to cry, but something was still missing, though. I must have been ignorant as to what *security* really meant.

The life I was living was not lining up with my missions, and it was eating away at me like a cankerworm. I was through with exploding and compromising. I could not continue to let my aspirations go down the drain because *we* were no longer on the same page. I longed to be loved with passion and support and not just with a *body*. I couldn't profess to be one way at Church but at home, not be the same. I still had children, who needed to see their Mother as a true disciple. Happy at home and at Church, *on both fronts*.

Suddenly, I began to review what was real and what was lies. I recognized the truth and slowly but surely embraced it. I prayed that things would change and that I would build tolerance. Then I gave ultimatums. *"In six months,* I proclaimed, *something had to give."* And in that six months, I *praised* and *pressed*. I wanted to breathe. I had had enough of bickering. I was tired of paying all the *larger* bills. Tired of going back and forth, with no signs of *growth*. I was even tired of *smoking*. I didn't have to get high. *I had a natural high*! I had to get rid of all forms of weakness on my behalf *first*.

I was content with the image of marriage. I failed to communicate fully what it would take to make it last. We needed more than just a financial need to be met… and while I didn't want to… it happened… I used my tax refund and paid a Lawyer to annul the Union. I was free! I felt like shouting from the mountain top… "*FREE AT LAST… FREE AT LAST… THANK GOD ALMIGHTY… I'M FREE AT LAST!*"

I was not proud that yet another relationship failed in my life, and I dare not say this one was something to write home about, yet, it was all I could do to keep my sanity.

The day came and went so fast for us to sign the papers, and yes, the tears rolled down his face, he pleaded that this was a big mistake on my part that my sons would suffer greatly without him in their lives. And maybe so, since it was after four years of courtship and one year of marriage… A decent amount of time to have someone consistently in my children's life… Someone who I never birthed a child from…. Someone who helped me get out of a bad state... Yet, the fact of the matter is, the damage was done, and the five years were NOT peaches and cream, we were just going *through the motions*. Co-existing. As a matter of opinion, it dawned on me in the process, I had never even been to a movie with this man, and neither had my boys, and that came to me when the crazy guy shot up the theater in Denver. Just to think that there were people there on dates, with their children and even if it was a sad ending, it made me think of the fact that they *were out together*, which means the *survivors can heal together*. A crazy notion, yet real enough to think and say "Hummmmm," it's just one of those things. I was no longer going to bite my nose to spite my face. I was an anointed Child of God, and it was my God given right to do what He wanted me to do, and not what *I* wanted to do.

When *G* couldn't get his way, he would try to turn the tables on me, make me feel guilty or if we didn't agree about a situation with my boys. He would say things like, "*I am not leaving you, you will leave before I will…*" But, I was not going to tolerate him raising his voice at me and all I could remember, during getting the divorce papers signed, is when he chose to talk to one of his family members back in VA. "*She changed when I got here… just like I thought… she holier than though now… I joined the Church, and she still wasn't happy.*" I ran into the living room, vexed… "*Who you talking to?*" and before I knew it, I had wrapped the telephone cord around his neck. I had sacrificed too much! So not only was I free… G *was too*.

Then it was my family's turn to turn on me… they were ready for me to move out of the family house because I had used my rent money to go and visit my real Mother in Alabama and didn't pay rent that month. They thought I was making it up… *Who makes up a story that your Mother had a stroke*?!? Well, some may, but I don't. So, again, I was looking for affordable housing upon my return. And I knew and trusted that a way was going to be made.

The next couple of years, from there, was a blur. I continued to work, back to two jobs again. One as a College Enrollment Representative, for my Alma Mater and the other for another local radio station, that wasn't locally owned. *Go figure!* But the bills had to be paid just as my life; *Christ had paid it all… He paid for all of the suffering I had to go through and that to come.* I vowed to serve Him if he granted me *His* peace.

**A Solar Moment:**

It's funny because…. when God truly has something with your name on it, there are things you must do and go through in order to conquer and receive them in full. And, while I have been in and out of different situations many times before, (some the same), I felt secure in letting go this one last time. I felt safe in not adhering to drama, and more than anything else, I knew I wanted more from God and He from me. I needed to be still and listen… I had no idea what to expect with my new transition and to be honest I didn't want to know… I just wanted to see how much I could trust Him.

# CHAPTER TWELVE
## When You Ask For Peace

I had a dream that came true… I dreamed of a fire, and it was of my boys, I even smelled the smoke, I smelled the fire.

I woke up and immediately knew something wasn't right. I needed to be home more, and as if it wasn't bad enough… I was preparing to have major surgery soon.

July came and went so fast. I underwent my surgery. It literally was my saving grace, a *hysterectomy gone wild.* Due to my C-section child births, I had gathered adhesions, and my major organs were latched together. Come to find out, inside I was so messed up, that they found diverticulitis (pile-ups), and cancerous tumors, but to me, the waking up and finding all this out was the real wake up call, that I needed. I could have skipped the two catheters. I was bare due to my kidney and bladder also being removed during this rebuilding procedure.

With time to recover in my face, along with all that I have been through, one would think I would take total advantage of the rest. Nope, I couldn't be still. I had children to provide for. I mean, my birth Mother and Stepmother, were unbelievable as one stayed for a month and the other wouldn't dare let me miss *not* one doctor's appointment. And they were a big big help.

But day by day, and month by month, I became stronger. I realized then that I was *more than a conqueror.* We say it, but the major surgeries proved it for me. I nearly lost my life, but God said, "*Not so!*" I had yet to move into my destiny. So, I began to look at life and *spirituality* a little deeper. I recall during this time, I truly believed that there was more that God required. I questioned myself, *"Why am I missing the mark and yet, not really finding my walk in line with my findings in scripture."*

I studied with my *home girl* from the *"Burg,"* who now lives in Hawaii, and from the holy days to the Sabbath, I saw earmarks that matched *His* purpose for my life, yet, *not* found in *mainstream worship.*

*Had this calling come to an end, or has what I discovered prompted me to reach beyond the veil?*

During this time, not only had it been blended with a change in jobs, but a halt within the four wall Ministry of dance. I teamed up with the Radio Station, once again, and the platform was to make the City, *'Our Sanctuary.'* The planning came with much preparation. And during this particular time, my parents decided to downsize their business.

So, as the months passed, the upcoming summer festivals swiftly approached. The month of my born day also rolled around... Yes... March 9th, (*the death of Biggie*). I still remember it as clear as day. I was still working for the college, with my long hours. I looked forward to Friday's. Quitting time was 1:00 p.m. But this Friday, was different, it was *my* birthday... what I call a *National Holiday*!

When I got home my Sister Tee and Bro Rob with his new little white chick *Lilly*. Yes, *Lilly White, we'd tease* had an apartment in the projects, and when they showed up at my house, I knew it was on and poppin'... I never made it to my door.

My sister knew we had three hours or more before the boys even came home, so to the projects we went. They were proud of the new table they had just recently put in the apartment and Rob was so *OCD*. Everything was so in place. The couple, *still new*, discussed how they were working on getting to know each other. We had great drinks and filled the air with *sibling love*.

Rob wanted to make sure I enjoyed my time, so we enjoyed one another until the minute I had to pick up my youngest son. Then the following weekend, I would soon be off to my yearly sabbatical... off to do '*ME*.' When I got to my room, it was set, everything I needed and wanted for the retreat, was in there, my friends and family really have always had a way of making this day special, and they knew that that was my last day last most of the month... I would be on vacation from then on.

That Tuesday, after my birthday, I was off to Cleveland for a Miami Heat vs. Cavalier game, and the next morning, I woke up excited to tell my co-worker and my siblings all about the game! Yet, for some reason, my dream that I had months ago, flashed before me again, *a fire*. But, I quickly brushed it off, I mean that must have been the trick of the enemy right? I wore my *Kaki's* and my white blouse, finally, yes, and my trench coat as it looked as if it might rain. Then I remembered I had to work in the field, so I called the office and explained to my supervisor that I will start at South Park and work my way Downtown, to pass out the new advertisement information.

When my cell rang, and it was my sister, I thought it was perfect, see we're known for having either lunch or breakfast together, to catch up on the kids, our parents and our jobs. So when I answered, her voice was low and sure... *her words still resound til this day.*

"*Nae, Lilly just called, and well, she said there was a fire at her house, and Rob was the only one there. Nae, they think he may be inside, I can see the smoke from here,*" were her exact words, but, we were all just together were my thoughts. Oh, oh okay... what do I do? My sister was accustomed to staying as cool as possible, but today, she said with a shaky voice, *"come get me now."* So, out the door... I flew.

When we arrived at *Pilgrim Village,* there was yellow caution tape, big fire trucks, police with ambulances surrounding the apartment and a quick flash of *Lilly* in a police truck, and this is when my heart stopped. It was as if my actual heart jumped out and read the yellow tape and knew it was important for us not to go any further. On the outside, I was able to dial my job, and with the most strength that I could muster up, I braced myself, and spoke to my Savior saying, *"Lord if you give me PEACE, I'll serve you."*

**A Solar Moment**:

The stronger you become… the more you will know that your position in life is important. And always remember, SHALOM (peace) is a *lifestyle.*

# CHAPTER THIRTEEN
## Through The Fire

As I paid closer attention, I noticed the firefighters kept away from us, and so did the Chief, but my vision became clear and one of the firefighters, I recognized. I was able to get his attention, and he slowly walked towards me... his words were slower than his walk, and he asked me a few questions, but all I needed to know.... *Was... was my brother inside of that apartment.* He kindly gestured that he was not sure, but it was believed that there may be someone in the house still.

Moments, turned into hours and before I knew it, my Mom was running up, my little brother was there along with cousins, aunts, and uncles. But, *no Dad! Wait... I remember now, he was away.* I hadn't called him yet. We were taught not to call each other with bad news when someone is out of town, but when my phone rang, and my Father asked me what was going on, I answered him. (I felt so bad for my Mom because she was here to face this alone, and not with my Father). No to mention, they were so close, and *Robert* has my Dad's last name because of the two of them).

The hours passed and breakfast became lunch, with no food in sight, but the fruit of love and support was there as we waited and the community showed up for support.

I will be honest.... I also can recall my supervisor, *who called and called and called*, which was not unusual in his nature, heck, while I was half dead after my surgery, all he could ask me about

97

were my numbers. But for some reason, I could not hold a conversation with him at all, on this day, so I called the office Secretary and gave her updates to pass along.

The moment finally came… where the man who looked as if he was on the golf course announced that the body found on the inside *was dead*, and just as fast as he drove off the inspectors were approaching the family asking who would be identifying the body. As the eldest sibling who heard her father wail on the phone hours ago at the thought of it being one of his sons, I rose to the occasion and was quickly shut down. My father's brothers did what our family does best, "*took charge.*"

My Uncle, the *war Vet*, would "*id*" the body and my youngest Uncle helped me stand my ground during this moment. Uncle Reg' was nobody's` punk and a man of leadership and catering (*a name that keeps my family name alive*)!

When my Uncle came out of the soot filled apartment, everything went blank. I saw my Mom just fall… my sister was a blind spot, and I lost all feeling in my entire body. *Not my brother, not in a fire… this had to be a joke.*

The days seemed to merge into one, and before I could fully grasp what was going on, we were lined up at a funeral, *his funeral… my brother Rob…*

I wrote a poem, and I muscled up the courage to deliver it. I know as we were walking in, I looked at the Pastor as if to say, "*this is a game changer,*" it felt as if God himself must have a direct message for me and was using this to open my eyes and ears. Well, *HE* won… and after the funeral, I slept for days.

It was almost impossible to go to work, and when I did, only my body was there, for everything I was asked to do, I gave resistance and attitude.

When I would get off, I would follow my routine and tried hard to snap out of it. I mean I had a lot going on at this time too. I was still dancing, but by this time, I was sort of on and off with going to Church. I had broken up with dancing (inside the Church) because my praise was not a ten-minute side show and I was also in a place in my life where I was questioning if I was really up to par with serving my God.

I had been putting off dinner with a DJ at the radio station, and even that relationship was straining me. I loved what I did and all the folks, but it offered me no cash, and I always would end up putting in more then I got out.

When *Boss Lady* called me that day, she must have known I wasn't feeling it, so since I had a little change in my pocket, I called and ordered food, rolled over on my bed and continued to cry. Once my tears even felt like they needed a break; I got up showered and made my way to work at the radio station. Then as if being there wasn't hard enough, the people, the same people I loved annoyed me because they kept asking me questions, and I had no answers to how I felt, what I needed or even wanted aside from *sleep*! I was still having mini fits of screaming and grinding my teeth, but with each day and each conversation with other people and professionals, I began making headway.

One day while I was working at a job fair, representing the college, I ran into one of our radio representatives, she was always a riot at the remotes on campus and so was I. We had a blast. I knew I wouldn't be at this radio station long because it used the community for their own gain but not *for the community.* It had not once supported the annual Juneteenth celebration in fifteen years. (I never had to worry about that with the #1 Gospel station, however). So, the festival tuning "40," I figured they might want to consider taking part before I knew it, we approach ahead Manager, that looked exactly the same as I remember *from* 15 years ago (when he fired me, to be exact, from being their receptionist).

Lo, and behold, within weeks, I was offered a job by the station and was really ready to get rid of the long hours at the college, so I took some time to see if I could first change hours, and be home more with my boys. My son had begun to fail in school, and my home was far from welcoming, clean yes, but ran by my children and whoever the sitter was of the day. I knew I had to be present for my precious sons.

With no choice in the matter, or maybe I did have a choice, but took the option to stop working such long hours... two and three jobs between the radio and my college and even overnights at the hotel, making reservations, just to be home more... *Just like the dream.*

During the time, I was still recovering from the loss of my brother but knew I couldn't sulk any longer, or it would affect my sons. So when I was invited to visit a new Church, where my niece attended, and also other students from the college where I had graduated and where I been employed, I jumped at the notion of maybe this way it. Their speech was different, I was intrigued and had to learn more and was elated to have been accompanied by a beautiful friend, Rachel.

My first visit into the Sanctuary was awesome! I was *drawn by the praise yet overwhelmed by the liberation*! What are the chances... I move to a new house, get a new job and finally, a new Church!

I had become sickened by what I called, *mainstream worship*, and had studied and prayed and saw more to the verse stating that

*"Christ came to fulfill the law, not abolish it."* I wanted to feel that *"He,"* being *"Christ"* would hold me to some higher standard if I am called by *His name*. And.... Well... I also had my Sista' Friend (who is now living in Hawaii) happy to share with me the truth about the Sacred name (that even had a deeper meaning and pronunciation), I was even the more determined to find if there was such a place on my quest.... In all places... in Buffalo, NY that kept *the Sabbath or the Holy Days*. I swore that there wasn't.

Now here it is, in this season, where I was withdrawn from the *feel good sermons*, and wanted to know the ways of the Apostles, that is what inspired "Making the City Our Sanctuary" citywide dance revival and lead me to redirect the extent of the Ministry given to me. I mean dancing and flagging is not show, it is a Prophetic posture that should be welcomed in the service of the Most High, I landed... covered from mist, dew and stormy weather!

The gist of this season of my maturing life is measured now by what enhances me and my boys, by means of what is pleasing to Christ.

**What you saying woman of God...**

"I had it all wrong. I was fighting the good fight of faith, yet never reaching the point of reality. I recognized that my life must represent truth to expose the false. I was looking for love in all the wrong places, and really expecting it to love me back.

**A Solar Moment**:

Take time off and properly review, "YOU." Open up the idea of success and opportunity will come in abundance. Make peace with those you may have hurt along life's paths.

# Epilogue

*Moving Into My Destiny*

**Dear Lord!** Oh, My!! Most merciful, gracious God, in you I have found refuge!!! You have shown me that you are able to be all that in your word declare You to be. A Potter who stripped me of all my worldly elements then took and rebuilt me. You gave me love and isolated me but not for an unworthy cause. My enemies became my instant footstool, and I stand upon You... *the solid Rock that is higher than I.*

You, Oh, Lord, blessed me with my needs and some of my unspoken wants, yet it all came in your season. And to you, I will give all the glory and the honor! Now Heavenly Father, as I stand before you today, I recommit myself to you, mind, body and soul. For you have given me the instructions I need to live here on earth, and the wisdom to get a better understanding of *self-growth and worth.*

As I continued to complete this manuscript during a twenty-way day fast, thank you, Lord, for touching my mind as I recall all the greatness of my trails, shortcomings, and tribulations. You helped me stay committed to listening for your voice as I entered into your presence full-time! And please, let my light shine towards the many homes that helped me throughout my journey, the homeless women at CARES Shelter, the men, and woman who have lost their lives to domestic violence, their homes, jobs and loved ones who may have suffered any ill will. Touch all the religious affiliations that I have encountered throughout this walk with you and bless the ministry where you have already made provisions for me to join at the end of my quest.

Because of that, today I am standing in truth, growing healthy relationships and allowing You, the Most High, to use me in various ventures of ministry. I am to the core still hopeful to one day be a wife, yet courting the idea of a successful me. Healing comes at a cost and a very expensive one at that. Knowing where the hurt comes from, can help us heal, yet we must be vigilant to forgive. Rather it's forgiving others or oneself.

Finding comfort in your uncomfortable season… I found that my growth came with a level of discomfort, and botched emotions, when I arrived at the place of refuge where you directed my steps. I landed upon "*The Rock*," where under awesome Leadership (someone who went to High School with my Father no less) allowed me to learn truth and unlearn error, through them (the Pastor and Assistant Pastor) God gave me after His own heart, (Holy days, His Holy Sabbath and His Sacred name). Thank you! The cost of keeping ALL of Your Commandments was a small price to pay to fill my collapsed lungs that were brought back by Your purpose.

I am "*Moving Into My Destiny*," amid being deemed a '*Conflict of Interest,*' at most. My Omissions have been made and "cast" into the sea of *forgetfulness* when you favored me to be *baptized* in the only name given unto men whereby one must be saved, '*Yahshua.*'

Months back, I recall hearing Gods voice for myself, telling me to stay still and to separate myself from unwanted pain and discomfort. That warning stayed with me throughout months of spiritual break ups that hurt worse than natural ones. I broke up with pleasing family and friends, and that of giving my talents to organizations that drained me of building personal support and resources. So into the labor room of life I go... assured of the enlightenment that will come out of the release (from bondage), with this "print...." Balance, truth, righteousness, and power.

*To God Be the Glory for the work He has done!*

Janate' "Solar" Ingram

The Author's surname *"Solar"* is just as magnetic as she. The definition denotes her quest to shine no matter what the situation or circumstance to illuminate a bright future. As you read her intriguing Memoir, it is her desire that you be enlightened by her meaningful *'Solar Moments'* that she shares throughout her work after several Chapters. Subsequently, she tried to suppress the glow for years, but the beam of the light that shown within her would not allow *"Cast Iron Omissions"* to remain seared.

**Solar defined**:
1)  Of, relating to, or proceeding from the sun.
2)  Using or operated by energy derived from the sun.
3)  To effect by exposing to sunlight.

# About the Author

It will not come as a surprise that this talented, spirit-filled woman of God, who bears all in her first novel Cast Iron Omissions is called '*The Communities Daughter*.' A graduate of Bryant and Stratton College, with an A.A.S. in Business Management, she has served not only her College as Enrollment Representative but for the entire Western New York community. For over 20 years, serving on the Board for the Juneteenth Heritage Foundation, as well as working in the area of Radio Broadcasting for major stations throughout her career.

Janate' Solar Ingram, lives in Buffalo, New York and is the proud Mother of four sons and two grandsons and unashamedly speaks truth to light as she shares her soul and innermost personal experiences to help someone else who has been afraid to take charge of their own life. She has worked hard to overcome alcoholism, depression, rape, incest and domestic violence and with the help of God became a victor!

Cast Iron Omissions is a powerful testimony of how a young Evangelistic woman came to grips with her mission to do her life's work in promoting health and healing. The Author is also a Co-Author in the book, Wounds to Wisdom, the Survivors Series and has penned several mini poetry booklets.

I am to the point where I am Cast Iron…

My heart has been warmed, my confidence is rebuilding, and my soul is welcoming the will of the Most High.

~Janate' "Solar" Ingram

Made in the USA
Middletown, DE
26 February 2017